The Art Of Purposeful Living:

**A Taoist Guide For
The Modern Age**

The Art Of Purposeful Living:

A Taoist Guide For The Modern Age

Lim Meng Sing PhD

Published by Brolga Publishing Pty Ltd
ABN 46 063 962 443
PO Box 452
Torquay Victoria 3228
Australia

email: markzocchi@brolgapublishing.com.au
All rights reserved. No part of this publication may be reproduced, stored in a retrieval system or transmitted in any form or by any means electronic, mechanical, photocopying, recording or otherwise without prior permission from the publisher.

Copyright © Lim Meng Sing 2022

ISBN: 978-0-6455864-0-4

Printed by ?? in Australia

Cover design by Luke Harris, WorkingType Studio

Typeset by WorkingType Studio

*Dedicated to the memory of my parents
with love and gratitude*

OTHER BOOKS BY THE AUTHOR

In The Footsteps Of Zen: The Path To A Calmer and Happier Life

The Gentle Art of Tao Leadership – A 21st Century Perspective

The Heart Has Its Reasons: Poems On Love And Life—A Personal Perspective

Journey Of The Heart (Poems And Haiku)

What Is Love? (An Experimental Project)
Originator, editor, principal co-author

Growing Up In British Malaya: A Memoir

CONTENTS

Prologue 1

Introduction To *Tao Te-Ching* (道德經)
The Classic Of The Way And Of Virtue) 9

The 300 Reflections 15

Acknowledgements 83

PROLOGUE

This book was unplanned. I have kept a diary for a number of years and it has been my habit to jot down random thoughts on various subjects.

In late 2019, as I went through the diary, I accidently spotted a number of entries under 'Reflections on Tao'. In fact, I had almost forgotten they were there. The years have gone by since the first entries and, on re-reading, they seemed to make sense to me and I was suddenly impelled to expand on the list. Three hundred axioms are contained in this book but my preference is for the word 'reflections' as this is a humbler word than 'axioms'.

Then, Covid-19 struck Australia in January 2020. Melbourne endured the longest lockdown of any city world-wide and being locked-in gave me much time to contemplate and write on the subject of Tao. Writing has given me immense joy and satisfaction as I have been able to turn this staying-in into something worthwhile and memorable.

That Taoist wisdom is profoundly relevant to our modern age and daily life is indisputable. It has been whole-heartedly accepted and embraced all over the world, not least by the Western world, and as judged by the ever-growing literature being written perennially on the subject and the trend shows no abatement.

The purpose of this book is to highlight, in an intelligible form for the reader, the main tenets of Taoism expressed by the three Masters – Lao Tze (老子, the Old Master, 6th –5th century BCE) the founder, author of *Tao Te-Ching* (道德經), Classic of the Way and of Virtue; and his two followers, Zhuangzi (莊子 369-286 BCE), author of *The Way of Zhuangzi*; and Liezi (列子, Master Lie, full name 列圄寇 pronounced Lie Yukou 4th century BCE) his work is under his name *Liezi*. Some parts of Taoism are not easy to understand and even the top scholars have not been in full agreement over interpretations. In this regard, those who could not read Chinese were in a less advantageous position and have had to fall back on translations of earlier writers who were Chinese scholars. Fortunately, despite this difficulty, the essence of the Masters' teachings has not been in serious dispute.

My intention of conveying the ideas in rhymed poetry form, in my view, makes easier reading as the original writings of the Masters, in lengthy prose form, are not easy to read and require much more time. Furthermore, the reader's pleasure is not affected by the obscure, metaphysical and mysterious parts of their writings. Any of the 300 reflections can be read at random to suit the reader's inclination and interest and they can be pondered on at the reader's leisure.

This may suit the busy, especially business people, parents, workers and retirees, executives who are usually time-strapped. The book could be savoured during a coffee-break in the office or between online meetings, during lunchtime or when travelling home by public transport after work.

Interested readers who wish to further their knowledge of Taoism should start with *Lao Tzu's Tao Te-Ching*, followed by *The Way Of Zhuangzi* and lastly, the writings of Liezi under his name.

The writings of the Masters cover a wide range of subjects, from the metaphysical, the mysterious, the obscure and even the mystical, to the practical, the pragmatic, the mundane, ordinary and also the down-to-earth. It is amazing that none of the subjects lacks depth or is unworthy of further reflection.

The list includes the unknowable, mysterious and metaphysical Tao (The Way); its namelessness and subtlety; the all-pervading powers of emptiness; limits of human understanding in regard to the Tao; the natural order of the Universe and its inherent charity, compassion, goodness, generosity, gentleness and humility; happiness and contentment by abiding in the Tao: the peril of following the wrong path; the doing-away of self and the danger of selfishness, pride, arrogance, over-confidence, impatience, rashness, greed, lust for power and position; the virtues of simplicity, humility, frugality, integrity, love and compassion, generosity, tolerance and temperance, contentment, cultivation of the self to gain insight; the wisdom of quietude, calm and restraint; awareness of harmful external influences; justice and fairness in conduct; right speech; abhorrence of war, conflicts, contentions, hubris and disputations; the futility of superficial and misleading knowledge; avoidance of struggle, strife and strain in conducting affairs by following *wu-wei* ('the art of achieving without struggle or over-exertion or over-doing/meddling); practice of *Yin Yang* to achieve balance and fulfilment (the whole fabric of all essence is created by these two polarities); the innate intelligence of a child; the oneness of all beings and all things; ethical leadership in general and benevolent administration in public office; the ephemeral nature of life and all things; flexibility, softness, openness, gentleness *vis-à-vis* their opposites; the folly and delusion of making distinctions, of having fixed and rigid ideas and opinions; the dire consequences of not taking necessary precautions, of ignoring details, of not being prepared, of not foreseeing the final outcome when making decisions and last, but not least, understanding and accepting death.

The modern world is an unhappy place despite rapid economic growth being achieved in past decades. Apart from wars, conflicts, violence, ideological differences, mental problems have been on the increase due to stress, drug addiction, domestic violence, competition, the drive for material success, loss of values, discontent and lack of fulfilment, a sense of helplessness and existential emptiness.

On the economic side, there are the problems of poverty in many countries, wide income disparities and inequities, homelessness, widespread diseases, lack of educational and work opportunities, child labour, disruptions to lives due to globalization, destruction of the environment and its attendant deleterious effects, corruption and businesses' unethical practices.

Empirical studies show that economic progress does not bring happiness – indeed it leads to greed, corruption and is the cause of much unhappiness. Clearly, a new mode of thinking is urgently required. Herbert Spencer, the great British sociologist, wrote: Science is for life, not life for science. Thus, economic progress should be for the good of life and life should not be sacrificed for such progress – the human dimension should over-ride progress and profits. If human values are lost, life would bear no value. This calls for ethical leadership, good public governance and responsible community consciousness. That is why the term 'Corporate Social Responsibility' has been coined and its principles are beginning to be applied to corporations with a social conscience. Businesses are not to pursue profits at the expense of values neither are they allowed to damage the environment in any way.

In many countries, unethical business practices have caused much misery to average investors by making false promises leading to the latter's losses – in some instances, people have lost all their life-savings. Under-payment of staff has run rampant and even leading banks and financial institutions have owned up in the face of class-actions. That private-enterprise is generally immoral and terribly ugly is not a far-fetched statement.

The above brings us back to the relevance of Taoism in a troubled, immoral, greedy and unhappy world.

Ancient wisdom does not die but lives forever as it bears on the most vital aspects of life:

happiness and contentment, integrity, love and compassion, humility, generosity, tolerance, justice, respect for others, selflessness and altruism, pursuit of truth and beauty, openness to higher values and the eternal quest of mankind for purpose and meaning.

Taoist principles have been successfully applied by leading corporations and have been shown to yield excellent results.

Even more important, such principles have enriched individual lives and helped many to find meaning in a troubled and unhappy world.

If this book can, in some way, help to achieve this, the writer's task will have been abundantly rewarded.

Introduction to Tao Te-Ching (道德經) The Classic Of The Way And Of Virtue)

This introduction will enable the reader to have a better understanding and appreciation of what follows in the next chapter titled THE 300 REFLECTIONS.

Lao Tze was the author of the classic *Tao Te-ching* (Classic of The Way and of Virtue abbreviated *Ching*). His school of thought is labelled *Tao Chia* (道家 The School of the Way).

Tao (道) means the **way**, *te* (德) means virtue or integrity, and *tao-te* (道德) as a compound meaning is ethics or morality. *Ching* (经) is canon or classic.

Ching is believed to have been written in 600 BCE. It is the most translated book in the world after the Bible.

Ching contains only 5,000 Chinese characters and 81 chapters, also called verses. Its wisdom is conveyed through many paradoxes and challenges the argumentative, disputative and logical mind; *Ching* advocates that we should transcend words, as thinking and articulating words tends to obscure, obstruct, falsify or even tyrannize. It is an invitation to treading another path (the *Tao*) to achieve clarity, insight and understanding, as every person has an inner self that holds innate and holistic wisdom.

In this wholeness, reality and nature are understood, not in fragments, but in fulsomeness and nothing is lacking. The *Tao* is a way of living in consonance with the universe which translates into the harmony of living with others, the environment and one's own self.

In harmony, there is no discord or conflict – life becomes a unity as the oneness of the universe; all that is, is a whole that embraces all parts. In a symphony, every note must fit the whole musical composition and what emerges is a perfect and blissful blend of sounds that transcends the language of words.

> It is easy to understand that such a mode of thinking and way of life is alien to and beyond the normal experience of Westerners

> who are used to the application of reason and logic as they travel through life. *Ching* then offers an alternative to thinking, feeling, doing and behaving.

Yin Yang (陰陽), *Wu-wei* (無爲 non-action), form the core of Taoism.

Yin is the shady side (the female) and *Yang* the sunny side (the male). In a broader context, *Yin* is associated with softness, passivity, darkness, the valley, the negative and non-being while *Yang* is related to masculinity, brightness, the mountain, activity and being.

Yin Yang is the genesis of all changes. Being whole, it is complete in itself and unchanging in its natural self. If the two half components are split, disequilibrium and chaos follow. They pursue each other and, in so doing, this gives rise to a new balance.

Yin is night and *Yang* is day. Herein is the interplay of the two forces. They are interdependent on each other; if one increases, the other decreases and thus the balance is maintained.

The whole fabric of all essence is created by these two polarities. In unity, the *Yin Yang* crystallises into correctness as it bears on all things and enables a person to derive a clear understanding of reality. Applied to human relationships, this balance enables a person to embrace another person's point of view. In this flow, all things merge in mutuality.

If one grasps too tightly only to one part of self, there would be a blockage and chaos would ensue. A great lesson from *Yin Yang* to last a good life-time!

> The term 'harmony'(和谐) is so powerful in Chinese thinking and philosophy such that it is often written in calligraphy and posted in Chinese homes.

> *Wu-wei* appears in Reflection 3 in the next chapter and reads as follows:

Wu is 'not'/'nothing'

Wei means 'is'/'the coming into being'

the sage knows *wu-wei*,

accomplishing without struggling

> In not forcing things, nothing is resisted and the outcome will be a favourable one. As such, softness, gentleness and flexibility will overcome the fixed, the hard and the rigid – this is winning without striving, fighting, struggling or coercing. This is the heart of the changeless and eternal Tao which holds everything together in its goodness, generosity, love and compassion and overlooks no one.

In a restless, confused and disorderly world, happiness is hard to find and the teachings of Taoism on quietude, contentment, simplicity, gentleness, altruism, compassion and love, living in harmony with the self, with others and the Universe, and the pursuit of a virtuous life continue to be a beacon to millions who are troubled, lost and unfulfilled.

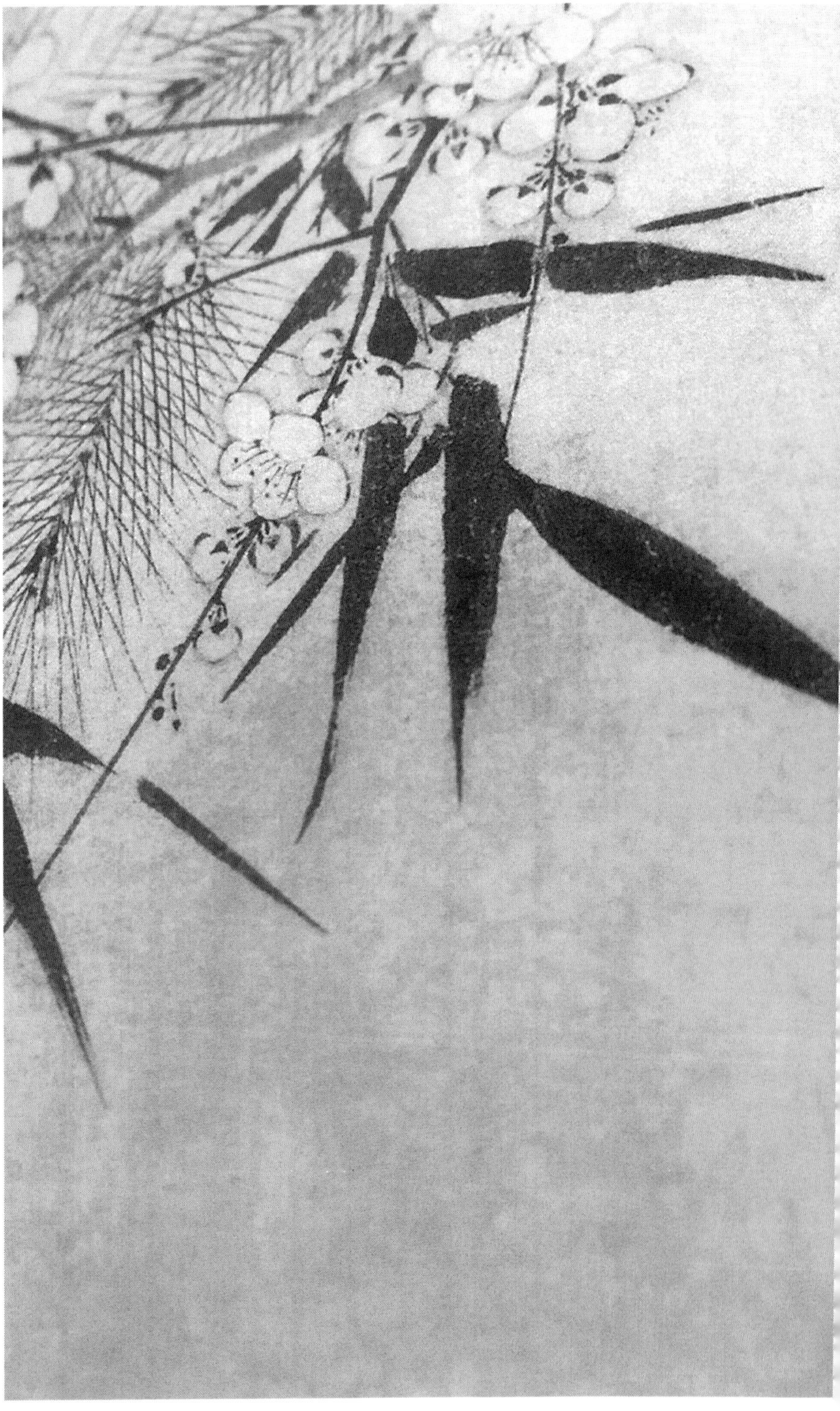

道

The 300 Reflections

1

In letting go

the Way begins

to show

2

The Tao cannot be defined

it eludes every definition

it is beyond the understanding of the brightest mind

3

Wu is 'not'/'nothing'

Wei 'is'/'the coming into being'

the sage knows *wu-wei*

accomplishing without struggling

4
Whatever that does happen
that faithfully follow
set free your heart
be one with the flow

5
This is the ultimate –
by what you are doing
stay centred

6
A path is made – to wit
by your walking upon it

7
Be generous in victory
that's the measure of your magnanimity

8
In seeking approval
yourself you chain
you have created your own bane

9

The wise sacrifice the superficial

for that which they regard as essential

10

Allow the heart to be free of turmoil

peace you would then not spoil

11

This is the just person--

all that he does embrace

is to give everyone their rightful space

12

If simplicity and integrity you embrace

you would dwell contentedly in Tao-space

13

Your essentiality

is defined by

your love of and concern for humanity

14

First fail that you might succeed

failure plants the victory-seed

15

You are appreciated

because you boast not –

as your superiority you don't display

acclaim is wrought

16

From you Tao does not part

when you walk in the ethical Path

17

The unwise pursue the material

the wise, the spiritual

18

If you must know clarity

first learn what is obscurity

19

That which is in Tao

endlessly does grow

those who walk its Path

such they would surely know

20

Don't over-use your garden

the best crops will not be begotten

21

Beyond your needs

do not consume

be generous

give others room

22

The expert speaker

makes no slips—he does not err

23

The sage needs no lock

as things he knows

 how to close

24

Those who are enlightened

insight they must first have earned

25

Intelligence is required, very much so

if others you seek to know

26

He perseveres as he is purpose-driven

he leaves no room for being indolent

27

Endure are these people as such

as they can uphold themselves in self-regard

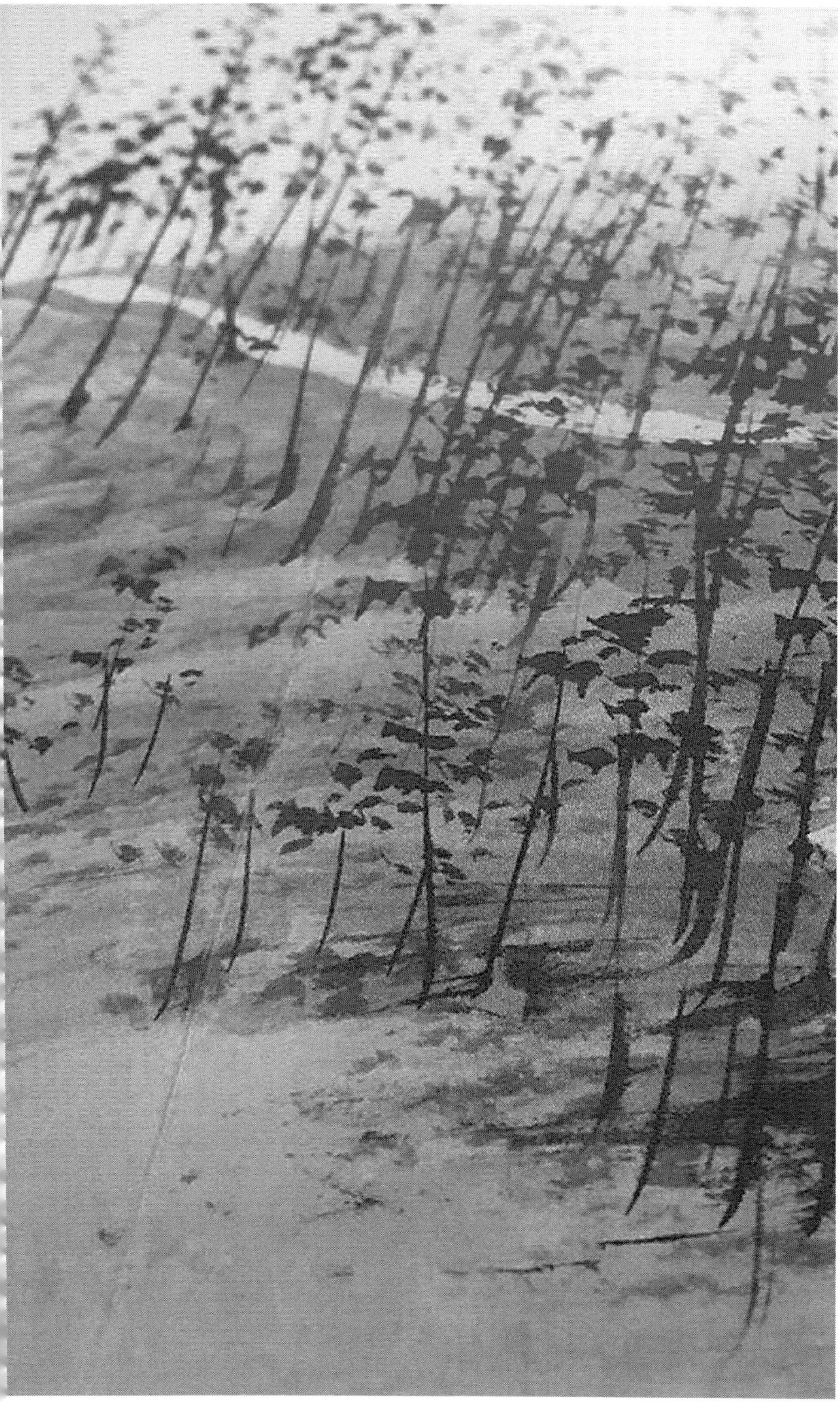

28

The high is built on the low

to be rooted with the common people

in sympathy, that the superior person does know

29

Self-centredness is not the trait of the wise

the very interests of others he does always recognize

30

The sage neither does grudge

nor criticize or judge

31

Knowing when to be silent

is the mark of those close to being enlightened

32

To govern, one needs

the skill of frying a small fish

the flesh falls off if over-done

that badly would spoil the dish

33

Knowing how

to untangle knots

is a skill known to very few

hardly in the uninitiated's thoughts

34

The superior person

knows how to blunt sharpness

in his sagaciousness

35

Tackle the task when it is easy

it would save a future of misery

36

Deal with a problem when it is small

this is a success-call

37

Be not deceived –

that which seems easy

might hide a great difficulty

38

Set order

before the appearance

of disorder

39

The first step taken

sets the journey

of a thousand miles –

this is basic Taoist philosophy

40

Impatience

lengthens the distance

41

The prize was missed

by so many

the realization was so close

but they were in too great a hurry

42

Be careful at the end

as the beginning

trouble would be averted

with such perceptive thinking

43

Knowledge does not wisdom make

the truly wise do not commit this mistake

44

This is the eternal message –

after their prime, all things age

45

They are one

the seen object and the beholder

there is no separateness

the connectedness is nature's order

46

The ignorant speak

though they do not know

silent are the wise

who are the ones who truly know

47

Cunning, cleverness, deceit

such have the lowest merit

48

The rich hanker

for more

they are unhappier

than the poor

49

A stumbling block

is the intellect

it dominates the mind

but insight it does neglect

50
People would not be willingly led
unless pride the leader has shed

51
In the leader's mind
the will of his followers
he never leaves behind

52
Such is nature –
things occur
as they must
without you lifting a finger

53
The Tao follower
competes not
he has sufficiency
in both heart and thought

54
This is the burden of excess –
sooner than later it begins to oppress

55
Being in tune with the Universe
the Tao-person achieves his purpose

56
He is reduced
as he is greedy
he who is generous
rises in integrity

57
Prominence is short-lived
the wise regard it as extreme grief

58
Those who are simple
set the best Tao example

59
Wise words have seldom been heeded

the inane many have preferred

60
Once you have caught the fish

you need not remember the net

once meaning has been grasped

words you can forget

61
The whole universe

to you will surrender

if stillness of mind

you are able to acquire

62
Discard distinctions

let the years pass as they should

plunge into the boundless

therein abide and all shall be good

63

People rush headlong

obsessed with happiness-seeking

direction they would not change

is this the route to happiness-realizing?

64

What I think

is echoed by the water

is this not a great wonder?

65

The mind of the child

is eminently sound

it merges in consonance with the surrounding

and moves along – ah, so very profound!

66

A quiet sleep is our beginning

and we die to a calm awakening

67

When the heart is steeped in what is right

'for' or 'against' falls away from sight.

68

Great wisdom in generosity always does well

contentiousness is what petty wisdom does spell

69

Beyond the sphere of knowledge

you should go

there is much more ahead

for you to grasp and know

70

Find me someone

who has forgotten every word

that I might converse with

it would be very much to my worth

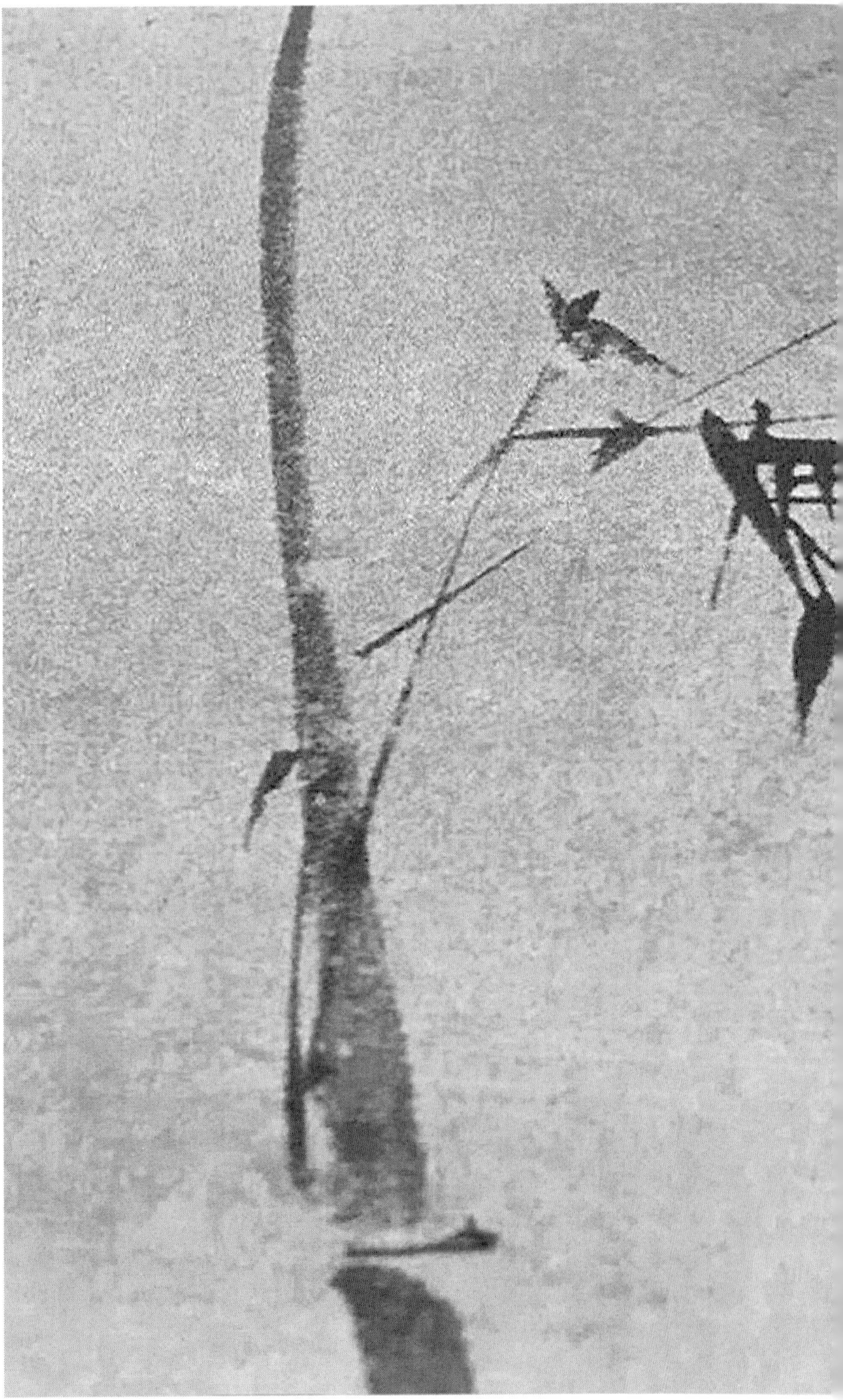

71

There are those who praise you

in front of your face

but behind your back

damning words find their place

72

The whole world

you might forget

but it won't forget you

a point for regret!

73

It is best when your understanding

does rest in that which is not in your comprehending

74

Tao does away with

affirmation and negation

as every such act does sadly lead

to inane single-minded attachment

75
Cherish deeply that which is within you

ignore the outside that will but lead you askew

76
Something worthy

takes a long time to complete indeed

a bad completion hits back

and cannot be remedied

77
If your self you have forgotten

you are ready to enter 'Heaven'

78
When a person

is not self-absorbed

the true forms of things will reveal

to him of their own accord

79

Not understanding is sounder than understanding

the former belongs inside the person

the latter is outside and could be the miscomprehending

80

Stand still in the middle

there is no need to hide away

or come out the self to display

81

Even understanding

can be deaf and dumb

bearing no worthy outcome

82

If the true nature of life

has been mastered (such people are few)

there would be nothing

to labour over what life cannot do

83

If the true nature

of fate has been mastered

there is no need to labour

over the knowledge that cannot be altered

84

They covered too much ground

returned empty, nothing of value they found

85

In order that you need not mend,

avoid breaking –

you would then suffer no bad end

86

Choosing the simple

is hard for so many people

87

As soon as a label is attached

reality becomes mismatched

88

Let your stillness

be like a mirror

such clarity

knows no error

89

The mouth of wisdom is shut

in squabbles it takes no part

90

Ignorance speaks louder than wisdom

no wonder so many are sadly trapped in that kingdom

91

You struggle

 because

 your thoughts muddle

92

Be like water

 you will not falter

93
To the Source
all things return
it was the First Cause

94
Be nothing
then you will be everything

95
Walk behind
others
wisdom you will find

96
Never mind the reason

just follow every season

97
Their coffers they filled
but such people were not fulfilled

98
How do you know
you know?

those who truly know

do not know they know

99
Leave behind the unknowable

speak not the unspeakable

100
Books too many

wisdom in scarcity

101
The star

knows not

it hangs away so far

102
The road

is neither broad

nor narrow

it's all in your rigid thought

103

Unbridled ambition-

the inevitable ruination

104

Smoke from your neighbour's chimney

why do you care?

If the house exists

it will be there

105

If you need to reaffirm

your ground is no longer firm

106

Go to the market-place

you will return with dust on your face

107

If nothing you hold too dear

where then is the fear?

108

Those who wear diamond and gold

their ego they have over-sold

109

When there is

there is the not –

nothing there is

if of that you have no thought

110

That which is struggle and strife

is against the nature of life

111

Things gather

then they scatter

the holding

is the undoing

112

You want to walk?

Stand then on your feet

don't talk

113

They live a lifetime

within a single day

as their heart is attuned

to the Way

114

Who can claim

to know the root

of Truth?

115

In not searching

the Way is clear

in intellectualizing

clarity will disappear

116

The most fruitful tree

could be the lowest

not the tallest

117

Information-full

makes the fool

118

Winning is not victory

if the victor has lost his humility

119

The greatest wealth

lies in frugality

it sows the seed

of future prosperity

120

Some day if not now

death is everyone's outcome

if you live in the Tao

there will be no fear or harm

121

The wise man

to learn he is eager

only the fool claims

he is clever

122

Heaven is high

earth is low

everyone they cover

though people's names they do not know

123

Only in the un-separated

is found the liberated

124

The cart too heavy

does its wheels break

excess is always a mistake

125

Beware – let not your seeing

become your self-deceiving

126

Losing or winning

means nothing

in the Tao of living

127

Sawdust drops from

the sawn-timber

all things in nature

they ultimately come together

128

A tiny thread

you should not denigrate

it could save your life

in some dire strait

129

The size of your glass

you should know

lest it ends

in overflow

130

Have no name

there would be

nothing to claim

131

They live

in another territory

but none need be

an enemy

132

Take not the side

of beauty

nor frown upon the ugly

recognize their propinquity

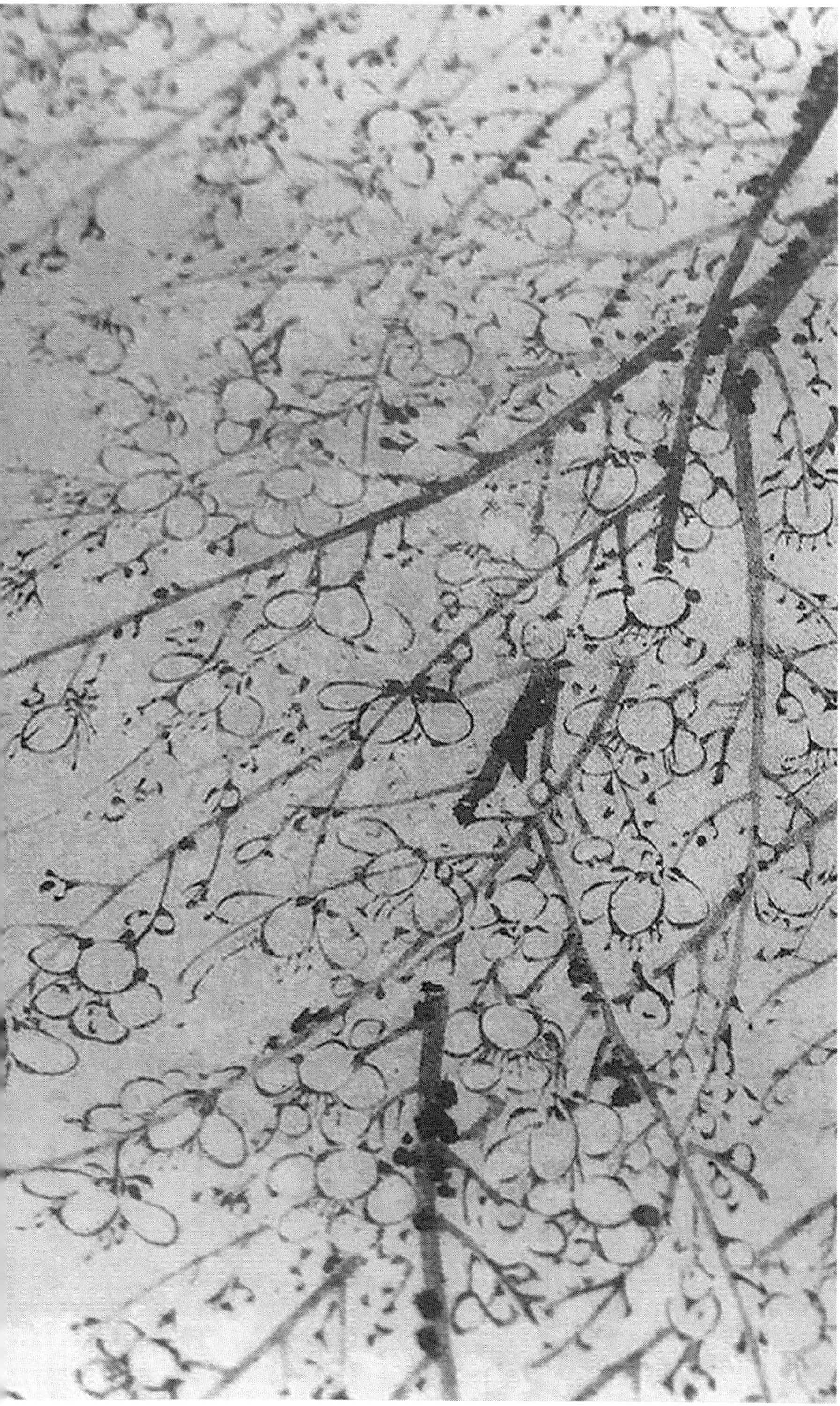

133

Hold to the Centre

you will never fall over

134

Mystery cannot be defined

none has the all-knowing mind

135

When the Tao you cherish

your total being It will nourish

136

Know your *Yin* and *Yang*

hold them in balance

all obstacles you will overcome

wherever your presence

137

You can't wish

the storm to go away

just stay

138

Little is not inadequacy

to regard so is sheer folly

139

Treat the small things

with reverence

the big things

will welcome your presence

140

The self craves for all

and is met with downfall

141

In giving generously

you will reap plenty

142

Poverty

courts no envy

143

Unless for the ripeness

of time you could wait

you would have no cause to celebrate

144

Contention is hidden agitation

145

Because the sage knows his weakness

he reaps the prize of success

146

The sage has a mind unfettered

his actions are unencumbered

147

Those who stand

in proper balance

do not falter

in any instance

148

Remove the self

do away with pride

in simplicity

and humility abide

149

Petty knowledge

blemishes character

petty conduct injures the Tao

and is at odds with the principles of Nature

150

The more the self-clinging

the further the Tao-distancing

151

Power and wealth

do not happiness confer

driven to excess

what it does is to smother

152

Both success and failure

they come and they go

the sage is indifferent

unfazed as he follows the flow

153

Self is burden

to the highest degree

a steel-clad prison

the source of endless misery

154

If you can recognize

the unimportant and superficial

you would know the chaff and the grain

coping with life would hardly cause any trouble

155

Be flexible in thought and deed

that is all the wisdom you need

156
The tiniest might hold
the rarest gem untold

157
Too many questions confuse
just a few basic ones, choose

158
How could the Invisible be seen?
To the Mysterious Void who has been?

159
The Tao is silent and calm but all-pervasive
if you do not assert, true wisdom you will receive

160
In your stillness is your clarity
there your mind should freely be

161

The over-hustled body

does quick fatigue court

with the over-worked mind

early exhaustion is wrought

162

Cultivate quietude and passivity

it will lead you surely to victory

163

Patient and aimless is the sea

yet adrift it stays – that you should be

164

How to bend and yield

that you should cultivate and know

be in contention with none

in virtue you will grow

165

People will recognize you, somehow, some day

when from sight your skills you keep away

166

Better to be deformed physically

than morally

167

Don't attract attention

you would know no contention

168

If you have virtue on your side

with the Tao you are already allied

169

The seasons know their coming and going

could you wait for things' settling and unsettling?

170

Self-mastery is preserved

when haste is unobserved

171

Eloquence

might not be the essence

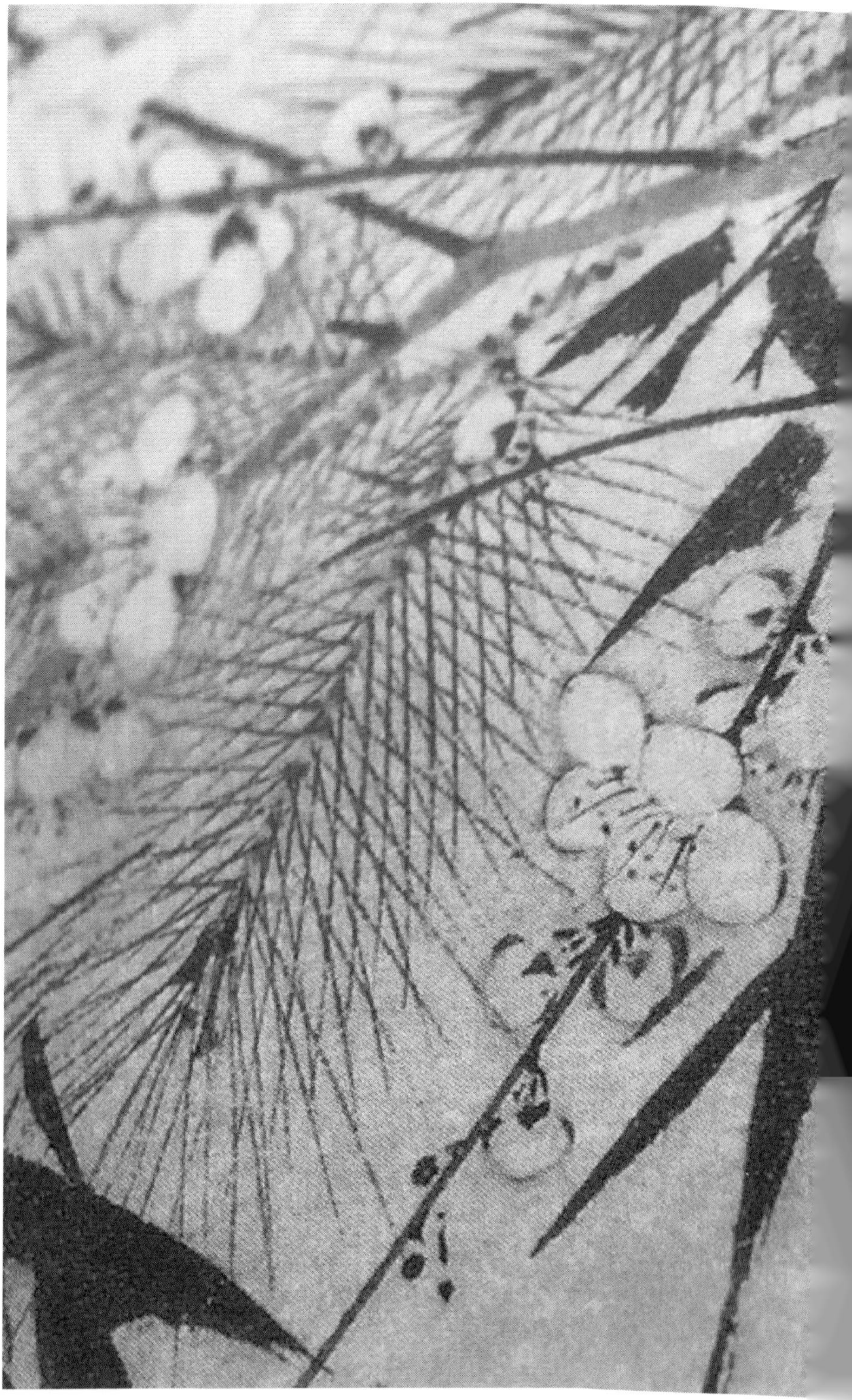

172

None does the sage reject

instead upon everyone he shows respect

173

Even from the bad person

there is to be learnt a lesson

174

The sage knows how to make

the useless useful –

uselessness is a desirable take

175

Let words be wise, though few

superfluity would but undo

176

Even a learned man could go astray

when from the virtue of Tao he walks away

177

Over-adorning does its beauty destroy

the simplest could be the greatest joy

178

Avoid force and arms

even in victory they cause harms

179

Even in life's roughest maelstrom

calm restraint would make for wisdom

180

The war is won –

is there beauty

in victory?

181

If yourself you know

you, none could overthrow

182

A thousand battles

you might have won

if yourself you have conquered –

you would be inferior to none

183

Be low like the depth of the valley

let that be the measure of your humility

184

The more to life you cling

the greater fear of death it will bring

185

The Tao denies no one

it accomplishes all

 but prides not what it has done

186

Great teachings, like great truths

elusive indeed they are

hard to grasp, but they travel far

187

If the impermanence is grasped

all doubts aside are cast

188

The sage's mind is mild

devoid of cunning – like that of a child

189

All boundaries are abolished

if your being is Tao-cherished

190

Not forcing, not meddling

is the route to accomplishing

191

A thousand names do not enable

defining of the Unnameable

192

Quietude and quiescence

is Tao's very essence

193

The beginning

leads to the ending

the ending exists not

without the beginning

consider them not as two

but just one thing

194

When the large

is diminished

it becomes small

when water evaporates

it becomes nothing at all--

nothing its permanence does retain

as there is sunshine, so is there rain

195

Strip yourself of desire

in your pristine simplicity, stay

detachment, calm and passivity pursue

that is the true character of the Way

196

Poverty does its reward bring

to nothing it needs to cling

197

Only those who are in harmony

with their fellow-men

will find Tao's tranquillity

198

Know when you should stop

you would then be able to stay on top

199

That which is already abundant

could be falsely claimed

to be inadequate –

truth has been maimed

200

There is no fear

with an open door

if there is nothing to hide

in your home-store

201

Mere adding to learning

could be the losing

as it implies striving –

letting go is the winning

202

The substance that is softest

can penetrate the hardest

203

Even without words

good teaching could be effected –

there is true wisdom in passivity

 such outcome would be celebrated

204

The mind that dwells in Tao

the entire world it clearly does understand

without having to pursue any knowledge

nor having to travel an inch to a foreign land

205

The sage never assumes

he is better than his fellow-men

he holds no fixed ideas or feelings

his ears to others he does lend

206

If life there were not

would there be death then?

Knowing their co-existence

brings fear of death to its end

207

The absence of striving for happiness

is the path to realizing true happiness

208

Words spoken do not for wisdom make

the ignorant speak but know not their mistake.

209

In the firmly-rooted

there great strength does dwell

wise are those who are prepared

such people will do well

210

Disturb not the natural harmony

to act against it is to court misery

211

Make no promise lightly

keeping it is a huge responsibility

212

If you could requite hatred with virtue

you would be among the enlightened few

213

To be first in the world do not aim--

in your humility

people would come to know your name

214

Two words does Tao disdain

'high' and 'mighty' – many people's bane

215

What is advantage?

what is disadvantage?

216

Let your boat be empty

no one will regard you as enemy

217

Intellectual knowledge – put away –

it is inferior to insight which goes a longer way

218

A frog in the well

cannot comprehend

the vastness of the ocean

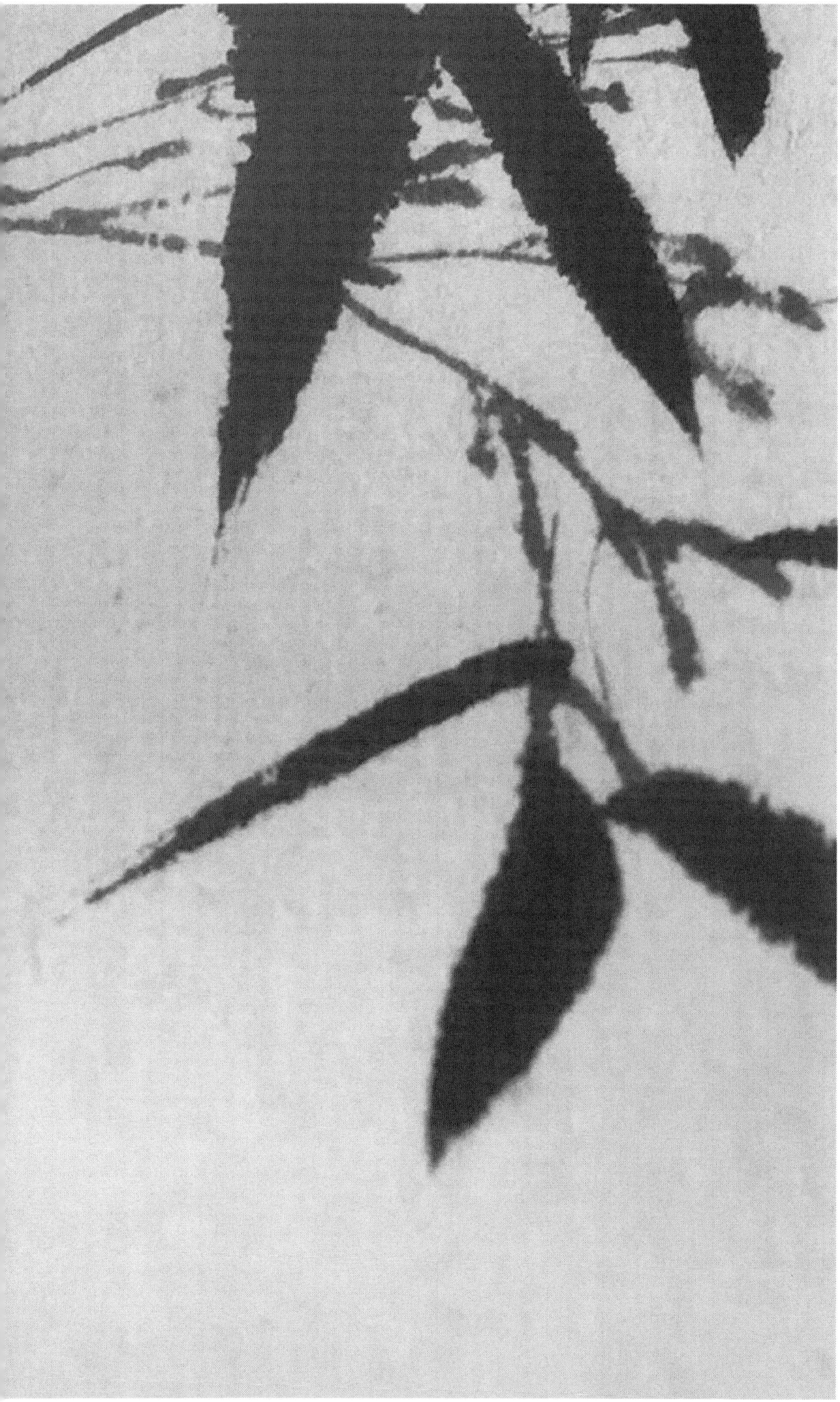

219

The eyes of the child see

more than the adults' clarity

220

The sage's wise words people shun

the foolish they prefer and are left undone

221

Love yourself – a fine thing

but don't exalt – that would be your undoing

222

Tao overcomes without strife

try apply this principle in your life

223

Prefer the soft to the hard

avoid the stiff and inflexible

also the headstrong and the stiff

success always belongs to the gentle

224

The poor the Tao

never does disregard

wealth it does not encourage

it has charity at heart

225

Which is better

fishing freely in leisure

or serving in the imperial court

craving favour?

226

The Tao is generous

no one is left out or kept behind

it is the Provider to all

it is ever compassionate and kind

227

To the undiscerning and uneducated

the sage's straight words seem crooked

228

Tao does firmly stand

on the side of the virtuous man

229

Fine words are said too often

but they are not true –

not fine-sounding words

carry weight but such people are too few

230

Bowing to social recognition

you end up an empty person

231

The blood of youth

is volatile and hot

such life lived in anxiety and worry

brings no peace of thought

232

Social gain –

personal pain

233

Two men in misfortune

one found himself in studying nature

the other lost himself in self-torture

234

Yielding is the way to survive

resist, you would court disaster in your life

235

If you are a slave to your mind

true understanding you would never find

236

Yield to others' opinions

you become the subject of their oppressions

237

Let your senses and mind be free

that is the route to liberty

238

Cultivate and nurture your life

all disputations but bring strife

239

The mind of the child

with the natural order it is in harmony

in its innocence and nakedness

it is the source of vital creativity

240

Your skills count less than your stillness

which is constant, steadfast and free from distress

241

Life is not about out-witting another person

this is the humble lesson one should learn

242

Reputation is only a visitor

those are wise who such abhor

243

Knowing the symptom effects no cure

know the cause and the problem will not endure

244

To win in an argument is no victory

it but leads to arrogance and bigotry

245

If you are self-sufficient

what more do you need for perfection?

246

Grounded in external affairs

you are consumed by society

anchor on your natural self

you escape the tyranny

247

Those who practise gentility are superior

those who live by force are inferior

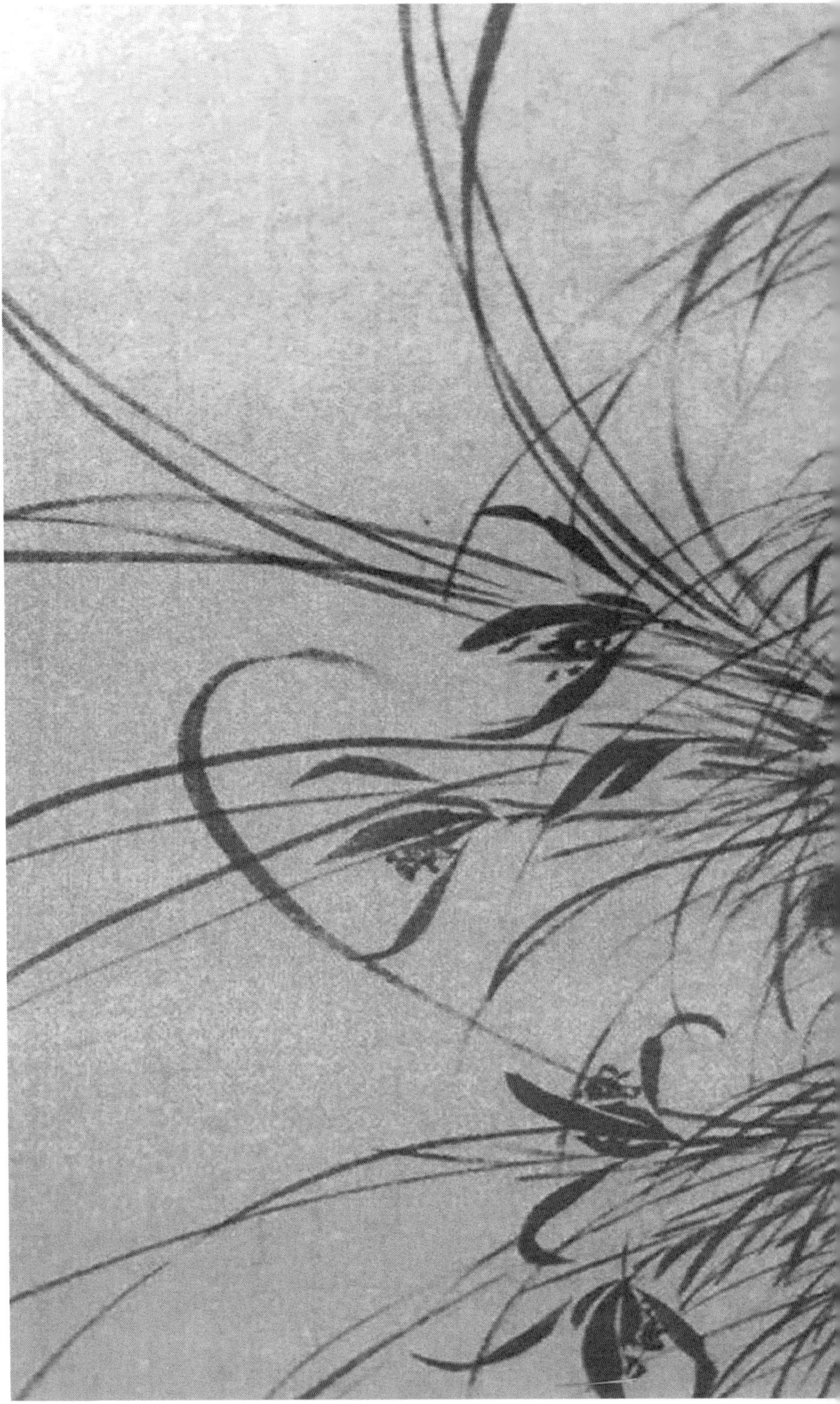

248

The person who lives with the natural order

has constancy of mind – never would he falter

249

Thinking that there is an end

and a beginning

is total misconception

250

When the senses

are engaged completely

the spirit rises

and the self dissolves naturally

251

Let life and death be their own

when there is life, do not hanker after –

there is time to embrace death when it comes

it is unwise to care for either

252

Knowing things directly

is superior to knowing conceptually

253

Death is rest and liberation

to the virtuous person

the lifelong labour is over

it is homecoming season

254

Do not fuss

all things appear

then they pass

255

Steel is harder than wood

but the latter has just as much good

256

External dogmas are to be avoided at all cost

cultivate your inner integrity instead

and nothing would be lost

257

Be serene, simple and natural

your life will be a miracle

258

Open your heart to the Universe

therein is your life's meaning and purpose

259

Words are inadequate to define existence

not even in their utmost persistence

260

Take all things as they occur

it is not yours to disagree or concur

261

Good government does not take its course

in either strain, restraint or force

262

Full it becomes

as it is empty – the Universe –

by its yielding, everything it holds

thereby it fulfils its purpose

263

Because the sage

does not regard himself as an end

himself he enriches

as towards that direction he does bend

264

Winning favour is dismay

it could be lost any day

265

The man in turmoil

to peace he does not endear

could he in patience remain

until the stream is clear?

266

The person is accredited

when no credit he does take

laying no claim, he is acclaimed –

in yielding, he does not break

267

To yield is to be kept whole

it will be filled – the hollow bowl

268

If faith you have little

how could you instil faith in people?

269

Kindling the self

does not bring any light

pride does not confer greatness –

such a life is never right

270

A sound man

can salvage anything

this is the consequence –

there would be no loss in this saving

271

If good is the speech

is there anything to impeach?

272

Among men the sage is the highest

as he is the humblest

273

Those who walk in the footsteps of Tao

are against conquests won by arms

weapons will turn against the aggressors

wars are the cause of calamities and harms

274

It has no beauty –

triumph in battle

they will not prevail

on the world – such murderous people

275

Peace comes to a land

when its members' coveting

comes to an end

276

Between what you are

and what you own

what would you choose

in your life's sojourn?

277

If you are anchored

at the centre of your being

even not leaving your door

you would know the world's every happening

278

Where would there be the thought
of death, if life (in the first instance)
there was not?

279

If you are not swept by love or hate,
loss or gain nor praise or blame
you will receive the highest acclaim

280

Imposing on others, that avoid
from preaching people, that refrain
they would then become themselves
pain would be averted and all is gain

281

The door to fortune might be opened by disaster
the latter could be fortune's harbinger

282

Love overcomes fear

give it room

those who such forsake

would court only doom

283

Action taken too quickly would bruise

grasping too quickly is to lose

284

There is no violence

in the brave soldier

there is no temper

in the good fighter

285

A foot behind is more desired

than a foot too far ahead

the former by the sage is preferred

286

The sage is coarse cloth covered in

his jade he hides within

287

Men should not be led by force

but by sanity which is the best recourse

288

Things that are supple and soft

bear signs of living

those that are hard and stiff

bear marks of dying

289

Weak is water indeed

yet untold power it does hold

the strong and hard it does defeat

over rigidity does gentleness control

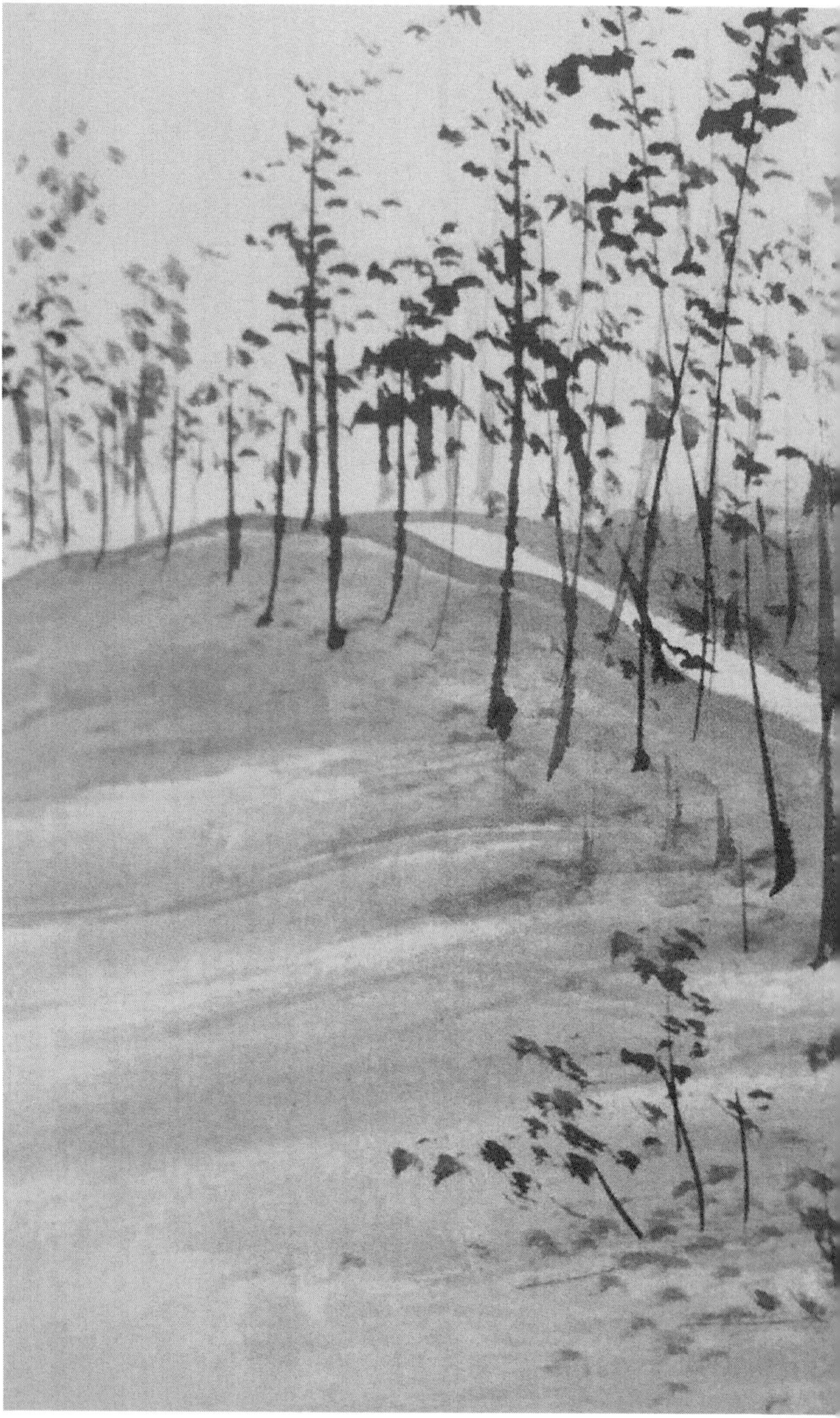

290

Patching up is the mark

of the virtuous person

attributing guilt and blame

is the personality of the villain

291

Magnifying and exaggerating

belongs to those who dwell in pride

in the diminishing and reducing

such people in Tao's humility reside

292

Life comes from earth

it returns to the home of its birth

293

The Way is meant for men

as rivers and lakes are to fishes

such is the natural order

and here truth clinches

294

Big is neither too big

nor is small too small

they are parts of dimension

with no limits as they include all

295

Too obsessed with winning

the archer loses his cool

in his shooting

296

It is not the ears

that give understanding

it is the heart and, ultimately

the soul, in illuminating

297

Doubts and chaos

upon such the sage does not frown

from such he creates

order and certainty, and wins the crown

298

When you seek to grasp

it slips away from your finger

holding to nothing and not-desiring

this is the sage's true character

299

There is no virtue

from those who

their ulterior motive pursue

300

Retire when the task is done

—this is the way of Heaven.

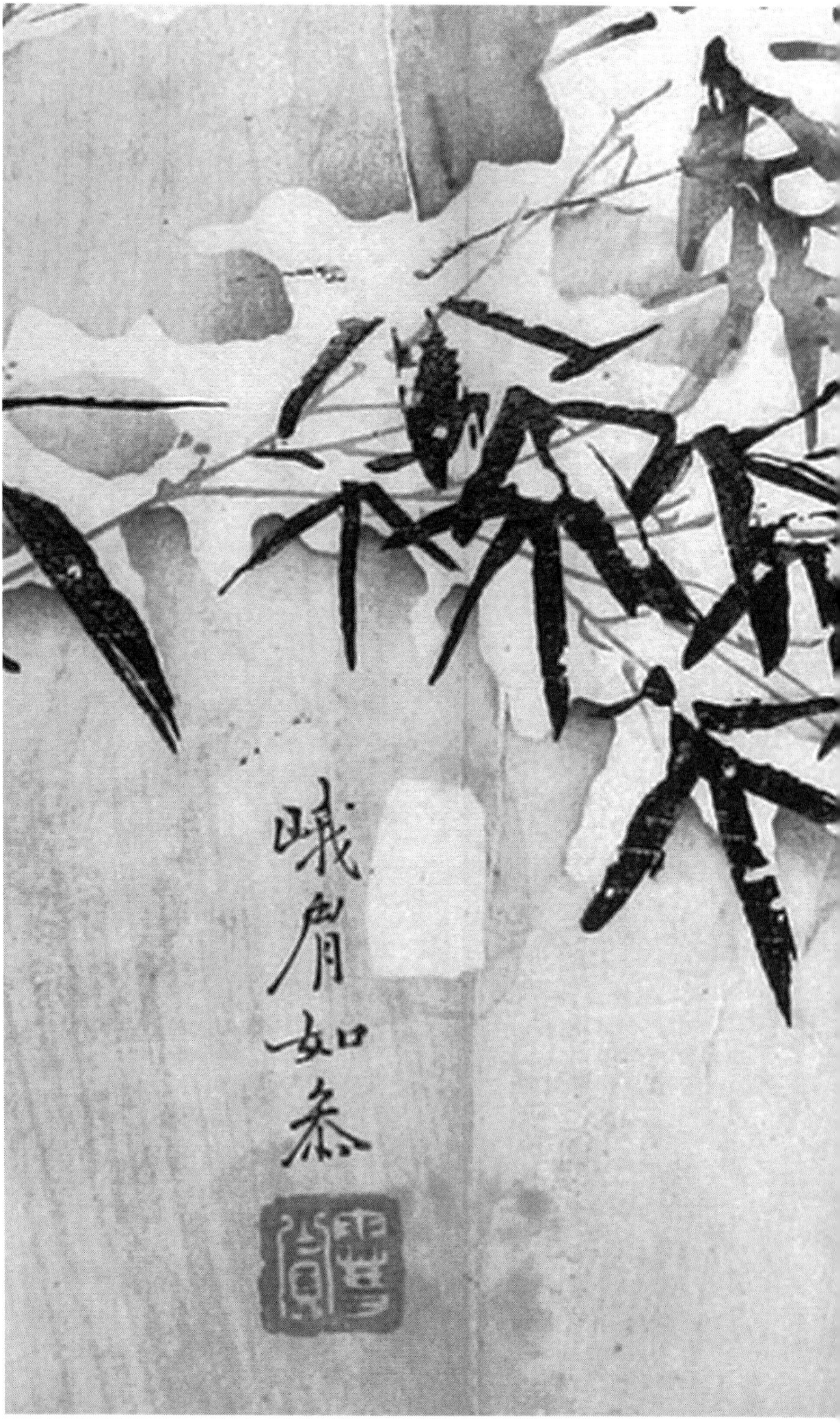
峨眉如黍

Acknowledgements

My wholehearted thanks go to Brolga Publishing Pty Ltd, Melbourne for its continuing support and encouragement since our happy relationship, which began in 2018.

I am particularly grateful to its editor Julie Capaldo for her patience, guidance and valuable advice to bring the book to fruition.

The success of every book is always dependent on a fertile co-operation between a writer and his/her publisher. In this regard, I am very fortunate indeed and look forward to continuing my relationship with Brolga Publishing in the years ahead.

I owe a great debt to my wife and my two sons for their unfailing faith in me and their unequivocal encouragement of my efforts throughout my writing career. This has given me immense inspiration and sustenance for which I will always be grateful.

Order

The Art of Purposeful Living

Lim Meng Sing

ISBN   978-0-6455864-0-4   Qty   ....
RRP   AU $19.99   ....
Postage AU $ 5.00   ....
TOTAL* $_____

* All prices include GST

Name: ....

Address: ....

Phone: ....

Email Address: ....

Payment:

❏ Money Order ❏ Cheque ❏ Amex ❏ MasterCard ❏ Visa

Cardholder's Name:...

Credit Card Number: ....

Signature: ....

Expiry Date: ....

Allow 10 days for delivery.

Payment to: Brolga Publishing Pty Ltd
ABN 46 063 962 443
PO Box 452
Torquay Vic 3228
Australia

markzocchi@brolgapublishing.com.au

Be Published

Publish through a successful publisher.
Brolga Publishing is represented through:
• National book trade distribution, including sales, marketing & distribution through Simon & Schuster.
• International book trade distribution to:
    - The United Kingdom
    - North America
    - Sales representation in South East Asia
• Worldwide e-Book distribution

For details and enquiries, contact:
Brolga Publishing Pty Ltd
ABN 46 063 962 443
PO Box 452
Torquay, Victoria,
Australia 3228
markzocchi@brolgapublishing.com.au
(Email for a catalogue request)